Acknowledgments

Firstly, I thank Prabhu Prasad Pradhan (@lensouledits) for designing the cover of the book. Without him there would have been no cover to judge the book.

I would also like to acknowledge my dearest friends Richa and Arzoo for instilling courage in me to publish these poems.

Lastly, I wish to thank my parents for constantly supporting me through this journey.

Poet's note

All the mentions of biblical characters are used as metaphors to represent the characters of the poem. They shouldn't be associated as mockery or harm to anyone's belief.

Contents

Her Perspective

"If only moving on was as easy as falling in love."

His Rhythm, My Heart

Is this what it feels like to be in love?
I could feel his words, a gentle touch,
Not just emotionally, but all above,
They wrapped around my soul as such.

His voice would climb and snake along,
Like vines that twist, both firm and light,
With tendrils that are soft but strong,
Ensnaring me in sweet delight.

And when he played his guitar,
The strings would hum inside my heart,
Each chord a beat, not far apart,
Our breaths entwined, no longer far.

My pulse aligned with every tone,
And soon, my heart was his to own.

A Sinful Serenade

I wish I'd never watched him play,
That sinister, mighty guitar.
He said he craved my deepest desires,
But all he found was himself in my eyes.

He loved me till my heart overflowed,
Filled me up as though I'd been void.
His touch, igniting—hotter than hellfire,
And when he played, darkness coiled around my heart.

I caught his reflection
And wished I hadn't—

It revealed the truth he hid so well,
A man devoid of love or care,
Scarred by wounds of past.
But still, I refused to run.

Dear Lord, forgive me for the sin I commit
Instead of devoting myself to crucifer
I, a sinner, chose Lucifer.

Mortal Love

God's chosen, the angel Lucifer,
Fell for a mortal—

Or did he feign the tender lie?
I, a fragile soul of fleeting breath,
Confessed my love beneath the sky.

And he, with arms of fire and light,
Accepted me, and worlds aligned.
The ecstasy was sharp and sweet—
Unreal, like a dream confined.

How could it be, this fated twist?
The mightiest angel bound by love,
And yet, he made me soar so high,
As if I flew with wings above.

Satan's Rebellion

Oh, how I curse the day I spoke my soul,
Forgive me for what I couldn't control.
I never dreamed the angel would break,
And pull me into his fiery embrace.

He swore to tear the heavens apart,
To wage a war for my blackened heart.
But God's wrath was swift and cold,
He commanded Satan to release his hold.

Yet he defied with eyes ablaze,
A rebel burning in Heaven's gaze.
I smiled, though darkness filled the air,
For in his arms, I felt no fear.

Not even death could drag us apart,
Not angels nor flames could tear my heart.

But his defiance sealed our doom,
And left him to face his fall alone.

Now I wear the grief like chains of stone,
For I am the reason my Satan lost his throne.

War in Heaven

The greatest war erupted there,
In a realm bathed in endless light.
They called it heaven, a place of peace,
Where every wish is within your sight.

Then why was Satan left bereft?
Why did love deny his plea?
Was he not worthy of a single touch,
Or the joy that flowed so endlessly?

The Archangel, standing tall with might,
Cast judgement with a blade of flame.
And who am I, a banished soul,
To place the weight of guilt or blame?

They crushed him as though he were dust,
Torn down like a faithless king.
For falling in love was his mortal sin—
And for this, heaven tore its wings.

A war was waged for a crime so small,
And left him broken, cast aside.
Was love, in heaven's golden halls,
So great a sin, they couldn't abide?

Fallen Angel

There he stood, my broken angel,
Wingless, dethroned, yet still sublime.
Defeated, but with power burning,
A force that bent even the strongest of time.

His eyes, like embers, blazed with wrath,
Yet hidden beneath was silent sorrow.
He ruled the flames, a king of ash,
But hell was just his cage to borrow.

He masked the pain with whispered lies—
"Rebellion was not in vain," he'd say.
Yet when his hand met mine, so cold,
I knew his heart had lost its way.

"My princess," he called, with voice so low,
As shadows twisted 'round his form.
"All of this, for love, was worth the fall,
Even in hell's eternal storm."

They named him *Fallen* not for his descent,
From heaven's grace to fire's reign.
He fell because a godlike soul,
Had given in to love's sweet pain.

Snakes and Snakes

I thought, how hard could it be,
To walk with Lucifer through hell?
A simple game of snakes and ladders—
With every fall, we'd rise as well.

Each moment with him felt unreal,
As if no serpent lurked beneath.
No hurdles, no venom in the air,
Just love, untouched by death's teeth.

But who knew the gods would spy,
Sending Lilith with her wicked gaze?
She caught us holding hands in sin,
In bliss beneath infernal haze.

She whispered secrets to the throne,
To the merciful god, or so they say.
He threatened death with a cruel smile,
If Lucifer didn't turn away.

My life of ladders turned to stone,
A game where hope no longer stakes.
For now, I see the truth unveiled—
It's only snakes, and snakes, and snakes.

Lilith's Envy

All because of Lilith's spite,
My love and I were torn apart.
She saw our bond beneath moonlight,
And poisoned Heaven with her heart.

What harm had we caused in the night,
To deserve His wrath and rage?
Our love, once burning fierce and bright,
Now locked within a gilded cage.

Lilith, with eyes like burning coal,
Grew envious of what we had.
She watched us, longing to control,
And turned her envy bitter, mad.

Her whispers reached the stars above,
A venom in the holy air.
She twisted truth and tainted love,
And left me drowning in despair.

She sought revenge upon our bliss,
Her lips were sharp with jealous flame.
For in my lover's tender kiss,
She felt her power turn to shame.

Why did she climb to Heaven's throne,
To break the bond we dared to make?
With every word her anger sewn,
A serpent's hiss in each heartache.

Lilith, a storm in silent form,
Her heart consumed with ice and fire,
She longed to make our love deform,
And see our passion soon expire.

Her shadow stretched across the sky,
As angels wept and turned away.
And with a single tearless cry,
She cast us both to Hell's dark sway.

Now, I stand lost in endless night,
My love's soft touch too far to find.
All because of Lilith's spite,
Her envy bound by cruel design.

Her jealous gaze, her bitter moan,
Has ripped my soul from love's embrace.
She, alone, now sits on a throne,
While I am left to fall from grace.

Rebel

The devil made his mistakes,
Without a trace of sorrow.
It wasn't just his devil's mask—
He hid the love he'd never show.

He gave up on us in a blink,
Before God could tear us apart.
Where's the rebel I once believed?
Where's the fire, the defiant heart?

If fear of God consumed him so,
Why take my hand in the first place?
The rebel I thought fearless, bold,
Turned out a coward, afraid of grace.

Manifest

I saw the signs, but turned away,
Blinded by the fire in his touch.
I suggested we fake the break,
But Lucifer refused—it was too much.

He whispered of risks to my life,
Warned that God would know the lie.
So he made his choice without a word,
And left me here, beneath the sky.

How could he abandon me, his peace?
He was my refuge, my only breath.
Now I stand forsaken on this earth,
Alive, but drowning in the death.

Why make me feel loved at all?
Why cradle me in warmth and light—
If he knew the heavens would crush us both,
Why did he give in to that fight?

Was I just a pawn in some cruel game,
A soul to play with when he tired?
Did I mean nothing beneath his flames?
Or was I fuel to feed his fire?

Do I not deserve love, a heart that's true?
One that wouldn't vanish in the end?
If only I had wished for mortal arms,
Not the great Satan, who could never bend.

Resentment

How can he ask me to simply move on?
How can he cast me aside so cold?
Was love just dust in Satan's eyes—
A fleeting game, a tale untold?

I wept and begged, "It can't be true,
I'm not afraid to face the grave."
But what I feared was losing him—
And he, too proud, would not be brave.

He pushed me back with careless ease,
Told me to think, to face the facts—
That God would tear my soul apart,
And angels wouldn't dare react.

The mighty Satan turned away,
Left me drowning in my tears.
How could he so easily forget
The love I offered through my fears?

The souls of hell whispered to me,
"He's always been this way—so blind.
No heart beats within his chest;
Love was never his to find."

How could I not have seen before?
The devil cannot feel or fall.
There's no damnation for his sins,
No justice in this hell at all.

But in my heart, where shadows dwell,
His name is etched with cold regret.

He will find no mercy there,
For I can never forgive—or forget.

How?

How can I move on, when every breath
Is haunted by his rhythm's cruel dance?
I close my eyes, and there he is—
A shadow, a ghost, a hollow trance.

How can I sleep when his lullaby
Echoes in the silence, a song of lies?
How can I pray to the god who set
Flames to the dreams in my tearful eyes?

I prayed for love, for something pure,
But it seems the gods and devils conspired,
Playing games with my fragile soul—
Leaving me broken, worn, and tired.

How could they ever feel remorse?
Their pride towers, untouchable, high.
My cries are swallowed by the void—
Lost in the dark where angels die.

How can I live without him near,
Knowing he was never meant to stay?
How can I breathe when every breath
Reminds me of how he slipped away?

How can I laugh when laughter's gone,
When he alone could make me whole?
And how, oh how, can I find peace—
When he was the solace of my soul?

Death

I see the path, the only way,
To free my soul from this thorned decay.
A life of pain, a heart in chains—
This is the choice, my only escape.

No other way can bring me peace,
But death, where all my torment will cease.
To leave this world behind, I'll fall—
And watch him rule, beyond it all.

The king of hell, with eyes of fire,
He rules the damned, the souls of sin.
What crime is greater than taking my life?
In death, I'll finally be with him.

I drag the blade across my skin,
Feel the warmth of blood begin.
A river flows, my final breath—
A smile forms, I welcome death.

No pain compares to what I've known,
The suffering, the nights alone.
For now, I'll rest in endless sleep,
And find the love I could not keep.

They say till death do lovers part,
But here, through death, I'll claim his heart.
In this dark place where shadows dwell,
Only in dying will we be well.

Infernal Embrace

My soul slipped from its earthly cage,
To wander where the shadows swell,
Through caverns deep and skies of rage,
I found my haven deep in Hell.

The stairway burned with crimson light,
Yet left no mark upon my skin.
The blackened gates loomed tall as night,
Inviting me to step within.

Around me souls in endless chains,
Their hollow screams a twisted song,
With demons wielding fire and pain,
Delighting in the wretched throng.

But high above, on jagged spire,
Where shadows kissed the blood-red sky,
Sat Lucifer, my dark desire,
His burning gaze met mine on high.

The Devil

They call him the Devil, and it's clear why,
A cheater, a liar, beneath a false sky.
He plays the lover, but it's all pretend,
A heart full of sin with no love to lend.

He faked affection, but what did he gain?
For lust, for power, my joy turned to pain.
I saw him there, on his lofty throne,
With a demon beside him, flesh and bone.

What was I, but a fleeting delight,
Something to use, then cast from his sight?
I gave him my soul, for nothing but lies,
Believed all the myths I thought were unwise.

His gaze caught mine, and his body froze,
But he let the demon's touch still grow.
He smirked, basking in my despair,
Revelling in how well he snared.

Now I know my hell, it's not fire and stone,
But watching my love turn cold as his own.
It's not the demons that tear at my skin,
But the memory of what we could've been.

Torment

How can I die again, I plead,
For my soul to end, to finally be freed.
To vanish from this twisted game,
While he revels in my endless shame.

He savours each second, each moment of pain,
As he dances with demons, basking in gain.
Their pleasure is his, while I stand still,
A silent witness, against my will.

A dagger, sharp, through my heart it goes,
As he lets their touch strip all that I know.
Once he was mine, or so I thought,
But in their arms, I see what I lost.

"My princesses," he whispers, soft as sin,
The same words once meant for me, now thin.
He looks my way to catch my fall,
And that is my torment—my curse, my all.

To see him take what I gave, forsaken,
My sacrifice—a love mistaken.

Days in Hell

As the days went by, my eyes ran dry,
Endlessly forced to watch and cry.
The same scene played, day after day,
No escape, no death, no other way.

Here's the truth that burned within—
You can't kill a soul steeped in sin.
I leaped into fire, but felt no pain,
Unscathed, I returned to this endless strain.

I begged the demons to tear me apart,
So Satan's betrayal would wound less my heart.
I tried every torture, every cruel game,
Yet still, my soul called out his name.

Chains wrapped tight around my soul,
Pulling me deeper into the darkened hole.
In mirrors cracked, I saw my face,
Distorted by grief, lost in disgrace.

And that's how each day in hell would pass—
A longing that outlived every lash.

Elixir Turned into Poison

He wasn't like this before,
His mouth, an elixir I'd adore.
Unbelievable, it seems somehow,
That the same lips spew venom now.

His hugs, his warmth, the sweetest bliss,
A tender back caress, a stolen kiss.
He'd hold me close, whisper "all is fine,"
Enchanting moments I thought were mine.

His words, once free of deceit or jest,
Felt so real, I thought I was blessed.
But I should have kept my feet on the ground,
And never floated where I'd be bound.

Dream That Burned Away

One fateful night in hell, a shadow came—
It was Satan, promising love in my name.

He placed a ring upon my hand,
His kiss, tender, as if planned.
Each moment slow, for me to keep,
A memory to savour, a love so deep.

For the first time, sunlight reached hell's gate,
Barging in, to bless our fate.
Angels and demons, side by side,
Showered us with flowers, love untied.

But then, my body began to burn—
The dream collapsed, and I returned.
Oh! Who do I pray to make it true?
To turn the dream of love anew?

When Did It All Change?

When did it all change?
Was it the day I cried, exposed,
When my weakness became his weapon?
Or the day I begged for a promise—
To never leave, or I'd die?

Did he tire of me so soon,
That I became nothing more,
Just an old flame,
Meant to burn out and be ignored?

Toy

I demanded an audience with the hellish lord,
But he refused—my plea was ignored.
Don't I deserve to know why,
What made him so quick to grow bored?

I gave my all, tried every way,
Poured myself into the game he'd play.
Is this the reward I earned in the end?
Oh, how I wish he'd just descend,

To speak the truth, face-to-face.
Until his lips confirm my disgrace,
I'll never accept that I was his toy—
His fleeting, discarded, forgotten joy.

Chains

The stone chains, fiery as flame,
No longer burn as they once did.
But one torment refuses to be rid.

I was his toy, a plaything of fate,
How can this bitter truth be real?
My heart was already his to break,
Yet he chained it, shattered what I feel.

These flames I endure with silent breath,
Yet the weight of betrayal is worse than death.
For in his grasp, I was bound,
Only to be cast aside, unfound.

Choice

I dreamt of ancient scriptures,
A voice like silk, a whisper so wise:
"Hell is not your punishment, it's your choice,"
It said, as if unveiling hidden skies.

In desperation, I asked with hope,
"How do I free myself from this endless night?"
The voice, a elixir to my wounded soul,
Spoke gently, guiding me toward the light.

"Change your choice, forgive your strife,
For taking the breath of your own life.
Forgive yourself, and you'll be set free,
The lords will forgive you, just as easily.

Then paradise, of your choosing and heart,
Awaits the moment you make a fresh start."

Forgive

"Someone tell me how to do it!"
I screamed, though my soul stood bare.
No body to hold, yet still, I felt
The weight of a heart beyond repair.

"It's not your fault," a voice replied,
Soft and steady, from deep inside.
I searched my soul for buried truths,
And realised why I'd truly died.

Hell was not for the life I took,
But for the guilt I couldn't release.
Subconsciously, I held the blame,
Chained to pain that wouldn't cease.

"It's not my fault," I whispered low,
Summoning the courage to let go.
I was just a fool, lost in love's storm,
But I don't deserve this endless scorn.

Then a light burst forth, blinding and pure,
The warmth of forgiveness, finally sure.
And in that light, I found my peace,
A soul redeemed, my torment ceased.

New Life

The light within me began to grow,
A warmth of wisdom, forgiveness aglow.
The thorny stairs of fire and pain
Turned to gold, soft petals in their reign.

The flames of hell had all but ceased,
Replaced by warmth, like a mother's peace.
The blisters, the scars, the wounds once raw,
Faded away beneath heaven's law.

No bruises marred my skin so pale,
My hair untangled, like a silken veil.
Dressed in white, a gown so bright,
It could blind the stars with its light.

I knew where this path would lead,
To the place where souls are freed.
From hell's torment to paradise's breath,
A new life awaits beyond death.

Heaven's Lord

I stepped into the so-called paradise,
Where God's smile concealed his lies.
The souls here wander, unaware,
Of the saintly mask he dares to wear.

He's the one who shaped my doom,
Who carved my fate and sealed my tomb.
Beneath his throne, truth lays torn—
The greatest God, a liar born.

Confrontation

I walked among delusional souls,
Lost in the grandeur of heaven's lies.
At the end sat the master of both worlds,
The one they called the beloved God, wise.

A flicker of recognition crossed his face,
Lucifer's old flame, now fallen from grace.
But the guilt he wore, a shallow disguise,
On the majestic face that told no lies.

For God can never be wrong, can he?
He'd never confess, never bend his knee.
Yet anger blazed within my chest,
As I approached, my heart unrest.

I felt the fury, deep and raw,
Ready to confront heaven's law.

Puppeteer

I raised my voice, a tempest unleashed,
"Your paradise is just a gilded cage,
A playground for souls you've deceived,
While you sit in splendour, a silent sage."

Shocked by the words from a mere soul,
He rose from his golden throne,
"Don't challenge the supreme power,
Do you really think it's all my fault alone?

I knew he would use you, it's true,
Tried to separate you both for your good,
But you, ungrateful, keep blaming me—
For your doom, misunderstood."

As his words sank in, the atmosphere changed,
My eyes opened wide, the truth rearranged:
Satan did use me, I finally see,
The puppeteer's strings were entwined with me.

Realisation

I wept as the truth crashed over me,
A tidal wave of sorrow, drowning my plea.
Used by my one and only, my heart left scarred,
Like a shattered mirror reflecting love marred.

I broke down, begging God above,
To forgive my foolish heart, my lost love.
His voice, a whisper, like wind through the trees,
Said, "I know what you seek, dear, if you please."

"You long to hear from Lucifer, bleak,
That you were just a toy, a plaything, so weak.
Bound in his game, like a marionette's strings."
I nodded in agreement, accepting the sting.

The King of Hell

He summoned Lucifer in the blink of an eye,
And there he stood, the master of lies.
No hint of remorse across his face,
Prideful and cold, in his darkened grace.

His gaze consumed me, devouring whole,
A silent torment, tearing at my soul.
I stood before him, shattered and frail,
Facing the demon, knowing I'd fail.

Lucifer's Triumph

I walked with trembling steps,
Toward the one I once adored.
"Why did you use me?" I asked,
"Was my love not a sacred chord?"

He chuckled, his voice like a dark sky
"The devil neither feels nor falls.
Love is but a fleeting lie,
A human folly that never calls."

"You, humans, are naive and weak,
Thinking you can make a demon care.
It was all an act, a simple streak,
To spark the greatest heavenly snare."

"I lost my wings but gained a throne,
Ruler of hell, power of my own.
I proved to the Lord and all his kin,
That a rebel's pride would always win."

"I used you to defy his might,
For it's God's wrath that fuels my fight.
Oh, how I revelled in your cries,
As you begged me, broken, under the skies."

"You, a child of gold, so pure,
Kneeling for love, seeking cure.
Through you, I showed Him defeat,
No power compares to my deceit."

"Now all angels bow to my name,
Lucifer, who played the ultimate game.

For God's beloved took her own breath,
To lie with me, the Lord of Death."

Final Sacrifice

His words cut through me, sharp as blades,
Like daggers forged in shadows' shades.
Each passing slice, slow to burn,
Carved through skin, making pain return.

My gaze then fell on the flaming sword,
Heaven's might, and final accord.
The blade that could end my endless strife,
I seized it from the hand of life.

I stabbed my soul, deep in its core,
Felt my essence bleed, forevermore.
And as I faded into the abyss,
I met the eyes of him for whom I risked this.

The one for whom I've died twice now—
First in flesh, then in soul's vow.
As nothingness slowly swallowed me whole,
I glimpsed in his eyes a fracture of soul.

As the darkness claimed my dying breath,
I watched his face, devoid of death.
A flicker, faint—was it regret?
A shadow of what he never met.

For in the eyes of the King of Hell,
I saw what no angel could ever tell:
Remorse, a sadness veiled in pride,
Emotions even Hell cannot hide.

And so I ceased, dissolved in night,
No heaven, no Hell, no guiding light.

But in my fall, I broke his wall—
A soul's farewell, the Devil's thrall.

Michael's Perspective

"I wish I confessed first......I wish I protected her."

Unrequited Love

How could I ever stop watching her?
Each time her eyes lit up with glee,
At every small and simple stir,
Her beauty pulled the breath from me.

With every beat of her gentle heart,
I found myself falling more each day.
As though the stars had played their part,
And made her my curse in every way.

Yet I had to keep my distance still,
For her love belonged to Lucifer.
And though it broke my stubborn will,
I watched them, knowing she was his.

It was agony, standing in the dark,
Seeing their bond that shone so bright.
But she alone could spark a spark,
In him, like daybreak after night.

Her laughter, the only thing to bring,
Joy to his cold and restless eyes.
And though I longed to be the king,
I knew in her arms, my hope must die.

Still, I could never turn away,
Though it tore my heart in two.
To watch her smile, to see them sway,
Was the only thing I knew.

Unseen Truth

I kept an eye on him, always near,
To make sure he would never cause her pain.
Her mortal heart, so soft and clear,
Too fragile to endure his dark domain.

Instead of worshipping her day and night,
He let his shadow turn away.
He betrayed her in the absence of her sight,
While she believed in him, in every way.

Oh, how I longed to tear them apart,
To save her from the lies he spun.
But how could I break her tender heart,
When to her, he was the only one?

I cursed the chains that bound them tight,
Wishing to shatter their cruel bond.
Yet to see her cry, I could not fight,
For her joy was all I longed beyond.

If only God could intervene,
To sever what was never true,
I'd watch her happy, pure, serene,
Free from the storm he always drew.

She fell for every lie he wove,
Her innocence, a light so rare.
Was her sweet love not enough to prove,
She deserved a heart with care?

But still, I watched in silent ache,
As Lucifer pulled her deeper in.

Her trust, her soul, he'd surely break,
And leave her lost in his dark sin.

Burning Phoenix

I tried to show her all the signs,
Of Lucifer's cheat and whispered lies,
But bless her heart, like stars that shine,
She saw only light in his dark eyes.

Her gaze was soft as moonlit streams,
Too pure to grasp the shadows there.
In love's embrace, she wove her dreams,
Unknowing of the snare she'd wear.

Was it her innocence that drew
My longing heart, like moth to flame?
Or was it fate that cruelly flew,
And bound her life to sorrow's name?

Her soul, as white as winter's frost,
Too fragile for the serpent's bite.
Yet in her trust, her heart is lost,
A lily drowning in the night.

But no matter how I praise her grace,
Her tenderness will be her fall,
She walks through fire without a trace,
Of fear that scorches, dark and tall.

She trusts an angel's veiled disguise,
A gilded mask of heaven's height,
Yet sees not through his fallen lies,
And follows him into the night.

The flames will rise, her heart will burn,
A phoenix lost without its flight.

And in the end, she will not learn—
Her wings are shadows in the light.

Dark Domain

Now came the time, as fates aligned,
For Heaven's hand to intervene.
How could I watch, with heart confined,
Her fall to Lucifer's unseen?

I climbed to God, my only plea,
To pierce the veil where shadows creep.
His anger, like the storm-torn sea,
Awoke from depths, long held in sleep.

How could He not, with righteous flame,
Protect the souls His breath had formed?
For man, His jewel, His sacred name,
By angel's envy now deformed.

Through Heaven's gilded gates of gold,
He soared, the light of worlds untamed.
His voice, a trumpet, strong and bold,
Summoned the one by darkness claimed.

God's presence was the sun at noon,
And shadows fled before His sight.
He broke the rebel's borrowed moon,
And cast him from the halls of light.

But Lucifer, with serpent's tongue,
Defied the order Heaven gave.
With poisoned pride, he lashed and clung,
Like roots beneath a hero's grave.

He stooped to show, with wings of night,
That darkness, too, held its domain.

And in the heart of holy light,
He sought to claim eternal reign.

Liar

Damn the damned, Lucifer,
For all the lies he spoke to her.
He whispered they were star-crossed fates,
Twin flames bound by Heaven's gates.

He sowed deceit like poisoned seeds,
And made her fight for twisted creeds.
Her heart, a lamb in wolf's embrace,
Believed their love was Heaven's grace.

He told her God would stand in way,
That angels feared their light of day.
With silver tongue and shadowed hand,
He wove her into his darkened plan.

She, the moonlight lost in mist,
A fragile soul by darkness kissed.
For him, she'd fall, for him, she'd burn,
For love, she'd let the world overturn.

But like the morning star that fades,
Her innocence in night decayed.
The light she gave, now lost, unseen—
A candle drowned beneath the stream.

Heavenly Battle

With no other way to set her free,
From Lucifer's dark tyranny,
She believed all lies but his,
A slave to his infernal kiss.

God and angels, torn by strife,
Chose to wage a war for life.
The only way to break her chain,
Was to cast the devil down in pain.

I, the archangel, led the fight,
Against the prince of endless night.
Our swords clashed high in Heaven's dome,
Our wings like truth and lies in foam.

In skies where stars could barely gleam,
We fought like echoes from a dream.
And with one swift, unyielding blow,
I struck his wings and laid him low.

Those wings, once bright with Heaven's grace,
Now tattered, fallen from their place.
His pride, his power, forever torn—
An angel shamed, a devil born.

His back now bled, where feathers lay,
And as they fell, the skies turned gray.
Weightless, they tumbled to the ground,
Yet in their fall, they made a sound.

A sound like thunder in the night,
As if the heavens mourned his flight.

And in that moment, she was free,
Released from his dark tyranny.

Blind Eyed Innocence

Why can't she see, why can't she know,
The Morning Star, once pure, now low?
He's cast from Heaven's sacred height,
A cherub lost to endless night.

His heart, once radiant with grace,
Now harbors shadows in its place.
The flames of Hell, his cruel domain,
Hold no love, only eternal pain.

Like Eve, she grasps the serpent's fruit,
Blind to the lies that took root.
For in his eyes, a fire burns,
A soul that God Himself has spurned.

No one can save her from this fall,
She walks the path of Adam's call.
Entranced, she clings to broken wings,
As Heaven weeps and angels sing.

Her love, a fragile candle's flame,
Flickers beneath his storm of shame.
Yet I, an Archangel in the fray,
Must watch as she is led astray.

But can the Devil taste of grace,
Or will he damn her in his place?
Will she, like Israel, wander far,
Lost beneath his darkened star?

For Lucifer, with prideful hand,
Now holds her life in shifting sand.

And I, with hope so faint and grim,
Pray that love might conquer him.

Lilith's truth

Then Lilith came, her eyes aglow,
With truths that only shadows know.
She spoke of Lucifer's cruel desire—
To use the human, fuel his fire.

She had heard him, clear as day,
When once she shared his darkened way.
Back when they danced in realms untamed,
Before the fall, before the flame.

He told her of his twisted plan,
To make a mortal love a damned man.
To prove to God, with mocking pride,
That he could bend a soul inside.

"She's just a pawn," Lilith confessed,
"A tool for his rebellious quest.
For he would show, in love's cruel name,
That angels, too, could stake their claim."

Her words fell like a serpent's hiss,
A venom laced in bitter bliss.
For now the truth was bare and grim—
The human heart was bound to him.

Masked Deceit

God's wrath burned fierce, no bounds in sight,
When word of treachery came to light.
His child, His own, a pawn in play,
Used in rebellion's dark display.

He called to Lucifer, stern and cold:
"Leave her be, release your hold!
Or face the end of all your might—
I'll break Heaven's law to set things right."

But the devil, wicked in his pride,
Spun his web of lies so wide.
He whispered, "God will strike you down,
If I don't leave, you'll wear His frown."

And so he left, with cunning flair,
Feigning love, a sacrifice rare.
But in his wake, he left behind
A broken heart, a soul confined.

For she believed he'd saved her soul,
Not knowing she was part of his goal.
Lucifer, coward, cruel and sly,
Escaped the truth beneath the lie.

Her Death

I hoped she'd move on, find her way,
After Lucifer left her in dismay.
I prayed she'd seek a love more true,
Someone worthy, someone new.
But never did I dream or fear,
She'd sacrifice all to disappear.

For him, the master of deceit,
She gave her soul, knelt at his feet.
She chose to fall into Hell's embrace,
For love that never held a trace.
Why did she end her life for lies?
Why did she chase the Devil's eyes?

I watched her fall—my heart undone,
And now I bear what can't be won.
If only she had heard my plea,
Turned away and set herself free.
But now her fate is sealed below,
A heart lost to eternal woe.

I carry the weight of my regret,
The fault is mine, I can't forget.
If only I had tried once more,
To make her give up what she adored.

Solitude

How can I ever see her again,
Now just a soul lost in Hell's domain?
I know her punishment—cruel and grim,
To see his truth, her love grown dim.
She must accept the bitter lie,
That Lucifer never cared, never tried.

Her torment: to face his hollow gaze,
And know her love was but a haze.
My only company is my own despair,
A misery too vast to bear.
I drown in sorrow, sip poison's wine,
Bitter and cold, like passing time.

Each sip reminds me of her fall,
Her death etched into my soul's wall.
This solitude is now my fate,
A life of regret, a love too late.
The weight of her loss pulls me down,
As I wear my guilt, like a thorned crown.

Her Final Sacrifice

I stood helpless as she plunged the flaming sword,
In love's name, she sought release from her pain.
But I, immortal, can never escape,
Only God can end my eternal strain.

Her soul drifted like stardust—gold and cold,
Fragments smeared on the blade, lifeless and bold.
Now I'm bound to watch her sacrifice fade,
A relic of love, smeared on steel, decayed.

I remain, cursed by time, lost and forlorn,
Immortal, but wishing I'd never been born.

Resurrection

I begged God to take my life,
To end my pain, spare me the strife.
Better death than to watch her cease,
Her soul now torn, my love in pieces.
But the merciful God, in His eternal grace,
Refused to grant my plea, no end to this race.

"Killing an archangel is a sin," He said,
"So live on, knowing she's dead."
Each day, a cruel reminder I must bear,
Her absence a weight too great to wear.

I begged once more—kill me or bring her back.
And the Master of All, with a smile that cracked,
Chose the latter, though worry lined His face.
He whispered, "Resurrection shall take place.
But let this secret never be unfurled,
Hidden from the eyes of the world."

Nothing compares her

The Lord Almighty paused before her resurrection and asked:
"What is it you see in her? Among Heaven's celestial host,
Why does your heart, an archangel's heart, bend to her will?"

I lowered my gaze and spoke:
"Her innocence is like the lotus, rising from the mire,
A purity that grows untainted, like Eve before the fall.
Her eyes—icy sparks—shine like the morning star,
A light that even the sun's glory cannot outshine.
Her voice, an instrument crafted by the divine,
Could silence the trumpets of Seraphim,
Her melody lulling even angels to awe.

Yet, beyond her beauty lies something deeper.
Her heart beats with the grace of the Almighty's breath,
Unstained by sin, unshaken by pride—
A love that mirrors the covenant,
And holds no judgment, no malice within.
She loves as Christ loved, with a heart wide open,
Seeing neither angel nor demon, only the soul.

But to answer Your question fully, I cannot.
She is my Eden and my exile—
The boon that lifts me, or the bane that brings me low.
She is both my salvation and my fall."

A Beating Heart

God took the flaming sword, its edge aglow,
Wiped the remnants of her soul, laid bare,
With mastery of power, the ebb and flow,
He breathed life into her, a sacred prayer.

As she rose anew, a part of me awoke,
For they say archangels lack the heart's embrace,
Yet in my chest, I felt the thunder's stroke,
A rhythm pulling strings, a fateful chase.

Back to Earth, she was sent, her memory erased,
A veil of forgetfulness wrapped her tight.
For ignorance, He deemed, was a gift, not waste,
To shield her from shadows, from darkness and fright.

I chose to watch from afar, a silent flame,
Fulfilling the fire that burned deep within.
To draw close would spell her doom, a tragic game,
For love too near could unravel the skin.

So I lingered, a guardian shrouded in light,
Bound by love yet chained by fate's cruel design,
Knowing her joy, her laughter, so pure and bright,
Was a spark in the night, a memory divine.

Alive soul

Her soul was vibrant, reborn anew,
A body alive, her joy set free,
No scars of sorrow, no trials to rue,
In her laughter shone the light of Gethsemane.

Oh, how I longed to whisper my truth,
To unveil my love, yet remained unseen.
A guardian in shadows, bound by my youth,
Watching her glow like the divine sheen.

From afar, I beheld her, a beacon bright,
Like a star in the night, God's promise unfurled.
Though my heart yearned to hold her, to make all things right,
I stood in silence, her protector in this world.

Shattered peace

Heavenly peace was shattered, Satan's gaze,
A mocking smirk, dark as the abyss.
"God's resurrected her, hasn't He?" he says,
My silence spoke what words could miss.

"Did you think I wouldn't know?" he jeered,
"I am the King of Hell, for Heaven's sake.
Life and death bow to me, nothing's veiled or feared—
What if I make her soul again quake?

What if I cast her into eternal flame,
Her love burning in endless pain?"
His threat hung heavy like the fall of night,
As Heaven trembled at the Devil's spite.

The Devil's Game

"She is not a toy to be played," I roared,
At the soulless devil standing tall.
He laughed, his pride like a sharpened sword,
"Do you not know, I conquer all?"

"My superiority knows no bounds," he hissed,
"I'll prove it by dragging her heart once more.
With a sly chuckle, he promised this,
"I'll make her fall, like she did before.

And with her pain, your torment grows,
For I know you love her—your weakness shows.
That's what makes me want to play,
To twist her soul and lead her astray."

I knew no words could change his course,
His wicked heart, beyond remorse.
Instead, my mission now was clear—
To guard her from his creeping snare.

Her perspective

"If only I was able to see through his deceit."

Shadows of Forgotten Grace

Parts of my memories, lost in the mist,
As though in a coma, long to resist.
Fragments of something I ought to recall,
Yet nothing seems altered—nothing at all.

But deep in my soul, a shift I can't name,
Like Eden's gates closed, never the same.
My heart beats with whispers of something erased,
A shadow of moments, too precious to face.

Why does it feel like a great storm has passed,
When the world stands still, unchanged by the blast?
Is this the weight of a secret untold,
Or the mark of a story that Heaven once stole?

A Gaze I Can't Escape

Why does it feel like someone's near,
Watching me close, yet I feel no fear?
Not strange or cold, but a touch I know,
A gaze that burns like an ember's glow.

These eyes, they follow with silent grace,
A familiar warmth, like a well-known face.
Each stare ignites the fire in my chest,
The same old yearning, that won't let me rest.

I can't explain this pull, this tie,
As if I've met that soul before the sky.
A watchful shadow, near yet far—
A presence like a guiding star.

Lucifer's Claim

Oh dear, there he was—those eyes I'd known,
A gaze that burned, like fire-stone.
A sophisticated man with power untamed,
Magnetic energy, my heart inflamed.

No heavenly force could hold me still,
His touch, electric, bent my will.
Even lightning felt ashamed,
Next to the spark his hand proclaimed.

He smiled and said, with a voice so pure,
"I am Lucifer,"—the name, a lure.
And in that moment, I was lost,
No turning back, no counting the cost.

Lucifer's Love

Isn't it sweet to be adored,
As if I'm water to his thirst,
The only cure to hunger's hoard,
But this love feels more like a curse.

His breath, once warm, now cuts like knives,
Each word, a blade I can't ignore.
Manipulation clouds the skies—
Why does his love feel like a war?

Lucifer's gaze, so dark, concealed,
A secret lurking in his eyes.
I sense the evil left unhealed,
A mask of love, a web of lies.

Fatal Allure

Even after all this pain,
Why can't I break this twisted chain?
My heart screams run, yet I remain,
Drawn to him, despite the bane.

A gut feeling whispers, deep inside,
That he's no good, no truth to hide.
Still, I can't seem to turn and flee,
Bound by a pull that's strangling me.

Attraction burns, but love feels cold,
My heart's not his, nor can he hold.
Why do I ache for what feels wrong,
As if I've danced to a fatal song?

He's not the one I'm meant to find,
Yet I'm trapped, my soul confined.
His presence feels both fake and dire,
A fatal flame, a burning liar.

Bound to the Abyss

Never should I have dared to pry,
To unmask the truth behind his lie.
Confronted by the devil's gaze,
The ruler of hell, set in a blaze.

His presence draped in shadows deep,
An allure so strong, it pulls me to keep.
Why doesn't fear drive me away?
Instead, I'm drawn, compelled to stay.

With every whispered, tempting word,
My soul is caught, my senses blurred.
He offers darkness dressed as light,
A false embrace that feels so right.

His laughter echoes, a siren's call,
In his arms, I risk it all.
Though I know the danger of his reign,
In his embrace, I feel no pain.

A storm brews within, a battle fought,
Desire entwined with the truth I sought.
Why does his touch ignite my core,
When I should flee, I crave him more?

In the depths of hell, where shadows roam,
I find a twisted sense of home.
Though he wears the guise of sin and strife,
I feel alive in this fractured life.

So here I stand, caught in his snare,
A strange allure I cannot bear.

For even as I tread this line,
I sense a bond that's darkly divine.

Divine Encounters

Lucifer was devilishly charming, it's true,
The master of darkness in a guise so new.
But one fateful day, beneath heaven's glow,
I met another, a light in the shadow.

With an aura like a halo, he shone bright,
A smile so pure, illuminating the night.
His vibe was soothing, a tranquil embrace,
Each word he spoke, a sweet, sacred grace.

We met often, drawn by fate's unseen hand,
His laughter like music, a soft, gentle band.
As our eyes locked, the world faded away,
In his presence, I longed to stay.

But soon the gaze shifted; we ventured beyond,
From fleeting glances to a bond so fond.
His name was Michael, a name whispered low,
A beacon of hope in a world filled with woe.

Tangled in Shadows

Michael was the friend I never knew I sought,
A soul so pure, in whom my heart found thought.
With him, I felt I could share my pain,
Yet words of truth slipped like autumn rain.

How could he grasp the chaos I bear,
This heaviness, this void that lingers in air?
A part of my past, like a ghost in the night,
Bound to Lucifer, hidden from light.

I tried to weave my truth in cryptic lines,
Metaphors laced with sorrow, yet so divine.
But he saw through shadows, piercing my disguise,
His eyes held concern, as wisdom arose wise.

"Leave Lucifer," he urged, with a gentle plea,
But unseen chains held fast, constraining me.
An ethereal force, a bond woven tight,
How could I sever the darkness from light?

His kindness an elixir, yet my heart is ensnared,
A battle within, where love feels impaired.
Michael's soft voice, a melody sweet,
But still, I'm tethered to the devil's deceit.

The Devil's Bargain

All my dreams came shattering down,
When Lucifer spoke with a chilling frown.
"We cannot be together," his words like a knife,
A mix of relief and a burdened life.

I craved his presence, a haunting delight,
Drawn to his darkness, yet shrouded in fright.
"Please, do not leave," I begged in despair,
But the king of Hell had a cruel truth to share.

"Kill yourself," he whispered, eyes glinting with glee,
"To be with me, embrace your decree."
A sinister bargain, a heart torn in two,
To dwell in his shadows or live without you.

In that moment, temptation's grip tight,
A dance with the devil, a perilous plight.
How could I choose between life and desire,
When love felt like ash, and hope burned like fire?

The Prince of Darkness

With anger etched deep upon his face,
He masked his true feelings, a twisted grace.
In a voice soft yet laced with disdain,
He spun his deceit like a spider's bane.

"God doesn't want me with a mortal like you,
But my heart is bound; this much is true.
If you die, then we'll reign hand in hand,
You'll be my princess in this darkened land."

Mockery danced in his haunting tone,
A promise of power, yet so overthrown.
To rule Hell together, a treacherous dream,
His love a facade, unravelling at the seam.

In his eyes, a tempest of conflict and pride,
An angel once lost, now a devil inside.
"Join me in darkness, forsake the light,
Together we'll conquer this endless night."

Awakening from Shadows

"Princess?" That word struck a familiar chord,
Each syllable dripped with poison, a haunting sword.
As he called me "princess," the past rushed like a tide,
Memories once buried now surged from inside.

I recalled the darkness, his games played so sly,
A marionette in his hands, dancing on a lie.
The truth was a bitter draught, stinging like fire,
Tears flowed like rivers, drowning hope and desire.

"You liar!" I screamed, my voice laced with rage,
"I'm not your toy; I refuse this cage!"
The veil of his charm began to fray at the seams,
And I grasped the truth woven into my dreams.

No longer a puppet in his wicked charade,
I'd shatter these chains, no longer afraid.
For his love was a serpent, coiled tight 'round my heart,
But I'd rise from the ashes, reclaim every part.

A phoenix reborn from the ash and the smoke,
In the light of my spirit, I'd shatter his yoke.
The crown he bestowed was a weight on my soul,
Yet I'd break free from shadows and finally be whole.

Lucifer's Ultimatum

I stood before him, shadow and flame,
Lucifer smiled as he whispered my name.
His voice was a serpent, smooth as deceit,
"Now comes the end where our stories meet.

I failed once before, when you slipped from my hand,
A mortal, untouched, in defiance you stand.
But no longer, your time has come due,
There's no escape now—I'm watching you choose."

From the darkness he summoned a blade forged in hell,
Its edge gleamed red with a sinister spell.
"The choice is yours—death is all I can give,
But how you die decides how long you live.

You can end it now, clean and fast,
Grip the sword tight, and your pain will pass.
Or leave it to me, let the torment begin,
And feel the slow burn of your every sin."

I felt the weight of eternity's stare,
Lucifer's laughter lingered in the air.
"You think there's a chance, a way to evade,
But I know your heart—your fears, your charade.

Kill yourself now, and perhaps you'll be spared,
From the worst of my wrath, from the fires I've prepared.
But if I decide, I'll stretch every breath,
Until you beg me, plead for death.

What will it be, then? Do you dare defy?
I've watched you suffer, heard you cry.

The time has come—your soul is at stake,
No more running, no more mistakes."

Michael's True Form

I ran through shadows, fear in my veins,
Hell's dark fire wrapped me in chains.
The flames danced higher, no escape in sight,
I closed my eyes, surrendering to night.

But in the depths, a warmth drew near,
A gentle light dissolved my fear.
Through tear-streaked eyes, I saw him there—
An angel, glowing beyond compare.

No mortal man, no fleeting dream,
His wings of gold began to gleam.
Michael, revealed in his radiant form,
Had come to shelter me from the storm.

"Don't be afraid," he whispered low,
His voice a calm, familiar glow.
"I've searched so long, I won't let go,
I can't lose you again to the shadows below."

His arms around me, my fear unwound,
In his presence, peace was found.
With Michael here, I knew at last—
The grip of hell would soon be past.

Battle of Life

The sky above me cracked with flame,
As Satan's roar tore through the night.
His eyes burned red; he called my name—
Hell's fury wielded in his might.

A sword of fire he drew from the deep,
Its blade alive with wicked fire.
"I'll claim this soul; it's mine to keep,"
He spat, his voice laced with desire.

But then a flash of brilliant gold,
Saint Michael descended from the sky.
With wings unfurled, his stance was bold,
His sword raised high, light in his eye.

Lucifer laughed, his voice like ice,
"Oh, Michael, you think you can save?
She chose me once, so roll the dice—
I'll show her pleasure, you offer grave."

The clash of steel split through the air,
As good and evil struck as one.
Sparks flew like stars, fierce and rare,
Their battle raged, far from done.

Michael fought with grace and light,
Each strike a blow to Satan's reign.
"For this mortal's soul, I'll stand and fight,
You'll never touch them with your flame."

With a wicked grin, Satan jeered,
"You think she'll stay? She knows my ways!

Her heart once yearned, and now it's cleared—
I'll win her back; this game's a phase!"

The ground beneath me shook with dread,
As heaven and hell clashed overhead.
Yet through the fight, I heard Michael speak:
"I'll not lose you to the flames so bleak."

The Mortal's Triumph

In the clash of steel, the battle raged,
Both warriors weary, their fury staged.
With swords entwined in a fierce embrace,
A moment of stillness in this dark place.

The swords fell heavy, their edges gleamed,
As darkness and light waged war, it seemed.
In that fleeting silence, my heart raced fast,
I saw my chance; I would change the past.

With trembling hands, I grasped the blades,
Their power thrummed as fear slowly swayed.
I plunged them deep, with all of my might,
Into Satan's back, a strike of pure light.

The cold steel pierced through his frozen heart,
A gasp escaped as he fell apart.
His roar of defeat echoed through the air,
The dark prince faltered, stripped of his flair.

With a final cry, his shadows receded,
The grip of hell weakened, and he conceded.
In that fierce moment, I stood my ground,
A mortal's triumph, in light I was found.

The Fall of Lucifer

In the depths of night, where shadows entwine,
A figure lay shattered, forsaken, malign.
Bloodied and battered, in darkness he bled,
The prince of deception, now defeated and dead.

With swords of light plunged deep in his breast,
The echoes of battle reverberated, unrest.
Once feared and revered, now cast from the height,
As Michael's might triumphed, dispelling the night.

His eyes, once ablaze with a merciless flame,
Dimmed to embers, consumed by shame.
The whispers of hubris now silent and stark,
As the ancient serpent slithered away, lost in the dark.

"No more shall you torment," the victory rang,
As the last of his power from his body sprang.
The wails of the damned now fading away,
A throne turned to ashes, in defeat he lay.

His laughter now stilled, replaced by lament,
For the light had prevailed, the heavens were rent.
The swords stood steadfast, a testament true,
To the strength of the Savior, and the love that we knew.

In this solemn silence, the world could atone,
For the choices I make, the seeds that I've sown.
With Lucifer fallen, a new dawn would arise,
As hope spread its wings, reclaiming the skies.

Confession of an Archangel

In the aftermath, where shadows fade,
I turned to Michael, my heart dismayed.
"Why did you save me from darkness and pain?
What love could shine through such torment and strain?"

He gazed with eyes like the morning light,
His voice a whisper, soft and bright.
"For you, my dear, I've fought through the night,
You are my heart, my guiding light."

"I've watched you struggle, your spirit so brave,
In the depths of despair, your soul I would save.
Though battles were fierce, my resolve held true,
For in all the heavens, my heart chose you."

He stepped closer, a warmth enveloped,
As if the stars themselves had celebrated.
"My love for you is a sacred decree,
A bond unbroken, eternally free."

"I could not let darkness steal you away,
For you are the hope in the light of day.
In every struggle, I saw your grace,
And knew in my heart, I'd protect your place."

Crossroads of Heart

In the stillness of night, where whispers reside,
I stood at a crossroads, with fate as my guide.
Michael's love, a beacon, so tender and bright,
Yet shadows of doubt danced in the pale moonlight.

A heart once shattered, now timid and frail,
Could I dare to love when trust had grown stale?
His eyes held a promise, a warmth like the sun,
But the ghosts of the past urged, "Run, don't be won."

With each soft confession, my heart swayed in fear,
What if the darkness returned, drawing near?
The scars of betrayal still etched in my soul,
Could I open my heart and let love take its toll?

His voice was nectar, like the gentlest prayer,
"I'm here to protect you, your burdens I'll share."
Yet doubt lingered, a shadow in sight,
Would I find solace or plunge into night?

Fate had bestowed this celestial chance,
Yet here I stood, caught in a trance.
Should I grasp the light or retreat to the dark?
In the depth of my heart, was there still a spark?

In the silence that followed, I weighed every thought,
Could I let go of the pain that I'd fought?

Guardian's Embrace

In the twilight's hush, where shadows play,
Michael sensed my turmoil, my heart led astray.
With a gaze like twilight, soft yet profound,
He whispered, "Take your time; I'll always be around."

In the depths of my doubt, his presence a balm,
A promise unspoken, a love pure and calm.
"I'll be your guardian, your light in the dark,
In this sacred embrace, let us ignite the spark."

With hands that caressed like a gentle breeze,
He pulled me closer, putting my soul at ease.
"Let the past fade away; here, you are safe."
In his arms, I discovered a warm, loving grace.

"Know that I'm with you, in joy and in strife,
With wings that will shelter, I'll cherish your life.
In this moment, surrender, let your spirit take flight,
For forever, my love, I'll be your guiding light."

Second chance: Embrace

With shadows behind me, and hope in my sight,
I felt the warmth blossom, igniting the night.
A decision unspoken, yet heavy and true,
To embrace the unknown, to finally break through.

In that simple gesture, a world came alive,
In the warmth of his love, I learned how to thrive.

A hug, a small gesture, yet vast in its grace,
A bridge built from trust in this sacred space.

As strong as Samson, with strength to defend,
With wisdom like Solomon, our hearts would transcend.

Like the dove of peace, sent from above,
In this embrace, I felt the depths of true love.

With each gentle heartbeat, a promise was made,
To cherish the moments, in light and in shade.

Like the faith of Abraham, steadfast and sure,
Love, once a whisper, now blossomed anew,
In the warmth of his arms, my spirit broke through.

Rising Phoenix

From ashes of heartache, I rise once again,
With flames of resilience, I embrace my own pain.
Like the phoenix in flight, with wings spread wide,
I soar through the darkness, no longer to hide.

With each trial endured, my spirit ignites,
Transcending the shadows, embracing new heights.
Born from the embers of struggles I faced,
I flourish like fire, in strength and in grace.

In the light of the dawn, with a heart made anew,
I dance through the skies in vibrant hues.
For like the phoenix, my journey's just begun,
With every rebirth, I shine like the sun.

<u>The End</u>

Everyone deserves another chance in love, a real chance to make things right. Breaking the cycle of repeated heartache is hard, but it's worth it when you finally do. No matter how good that cycle may seem from the outside—how comfortable, how familiar—it's crucial to take a step back. Give yourself time, ask yourself if it truly aligns with what you need deep down. Don't settle for something that's almost right, or just a bit less than you deserve. If it's true love, it won't leave you questioning. The right love is meant to stay, not just pass through. Trust that you're worthy of finding it.